Every day, after school, M
love to listen to their grand
She tells stories about the Hindu gods – a
monkey general, an elephant-headed god
and a boy with stars in his mouth ...

The Boy with Stars in His Mouth

"Everyone loves Lord Krishna," says grandmother. "That's why we worship Krishna at our family shrine."

When Krishna was a boy, he and his brother, Balarama, loved to play in the forest with their friends. They climbed trees, played hiding games and had races with each other. Sometimes, like all brothers and sisters, Krishna and Balarama argued with each other.

One day, Balarama ran home to his mother to tell tales.

"Do you know what Krishna is doing?" Balarama cried. "He is eating earth!"

"Krishna, come here," called Yashoda his mother. "Open your mouth and let me see inside."

When Krishna opened his mouth, Yashoda could not believe her eyes!

There, inside Krishna's mouth, Yashoda could see the sun, the moon, the stars and the planets. She could see the earth, the seas, the fire and the air – the whole of creation!

Yashoda knew that Krishna was no ordinary boy, he was special – he was God!

The Elephant-Headed God

"If you have a problem," says grandmother, "say a prayer to Ganesh. He is a wise god and like all elephants, he can remove any problem that gets in his way."

Parvati wanted a child, so she took some soap, mixed it with flakes of her own skin and moulded it into a baby. Then she breathed into its mouth, and Ganesh was born!

Lord Shiva, Parvati's husband, was a great god. He was busy travelling the earth, looking after the world he had created. He did not see his son grow up.

One day, Parvati was having a bath and Ganesh was on guard outside.
Lord Shiva arrived home and tried to enter the palace.
Ganesh did not recognise his father and would not let him come in.

Lord Shiva was so angry that he turned his third eye, the powerful eye in the middle of his forehead, towards Ganesh. Immediately, Ganesh's head was struck off!

When she saw what had happened to her son, Parvati was upset – and angry.

"Don't worry," said Lord Shiva. "Ganesh will have another head."

He sent his servant to search for a new head for his son. Soon the servant returned with the head of a baby elephant and Lord Shiva placed it on the head of his son.

Now both Parvati *and* Lord Shiva had created their son.

Parvati was happy. She thought Ganesh looked beautiful – and with his elephant head, he would be wise and strong.

The Monkey General

Most monkeys are cheeky and playful, but Hanuman is strong and helpful …

Hanuman's father was Lord of the Winds, so Hanuman could fly fast and far around the world.

When Rama was fighting Ravana, the demon with ten heads, Hanuman asked all the animals in the forest to make an army to help Rama. It was a fierce battle and soon many monkeys and bears lay wounded on the battlefield.

Hanuman looked at his friends and tears fell down his furry cheeks.

Suddenly he heard Jambavan, the wounded bear king, whisper, "Hanuman, fly to the medicine mountain and find the special herbs that will heal us."

Hanuman flew fast until he found the mountain with the herbs shining in the moonlight. He did not know which herbs to pick, so, with all his strength, he lifted the whole mountain on to his shoulders.

As the sweet smell of the healing herbs filled the air, the wounded monkeys and bears began to feel better.

Soon, the animal army was ready to fight the demon Ravana again – all thanks to Hanuman!

Can you tell a story about a Hindu god? Which story is your favourite?

Published by RMEP (Religious and Moral Education Press)
An imprint of Hymns Ancient and Modern Ltd (a registered charity)
St Mary's Works, St Mary's Plain, Norwich, Norfolk NR3 3BH

Copyright © Lynne Broadbent and John Logan 2009

Lynne Broadbent and John Logan have asserted their right under the Copyright, Designs and Patents Act, 1988, to be identified as Authors of this Work.

All rights reserved. No part of this publication may be reproduced, stored in a retrieval system, or transmitted, in any form or by any means, electronic, electrostatic, magnetic tape, mechanical, photocopying, recording or otherwise, without permission in writing from the publishers.

First published 2009

ISBN 978-1-85175-367-3

Designed and typeset by Topics – The Creative Partnership, Exeter
Printed in Great Britain by Halston & Co. Ltd, Amersham, Bucks